# Ciphers
## AND Codes

KAREN PRICE HOSSELL

Heinemann Library
Chicago, Illinois

© 2003 Heinemann Library
a division of Reed Elsevier Inc.
Chicago, Illinois

Customer Service 888-454-2279

Visit our website at www.heinemannlibrary.com

Page Layout by Vicki Fischman
Photo research by Amor Montes de Oca
Printed and bound in the United States by Lake Book Manufacturing, Inc.

07 06 05 04
10 9 8 7 6 5 4 3 2

**Library of Congress Cataloging-in-Publication Data**

Price Hossell, Karen, 1957-
  Ciphers and codes / Karen Price Hossell.
    p. cm. -- (Communicating)
Summary: Presents an overview of various types of codes and ciphers used throughout history, famous cryptologists, and how to create your own secret messages.
Includes bibliographical references and index.
  ISBN 1-58810-484-2 (HC), 1-58810-940-2 (Pbk.)
  1. Cryptography--Juvenile literature. 2. Ciphers--Juvenile literature. [1. Cryptography. 2. Ciphers.] I. Title. II. Series.
  Z103.3 .P74 2002
  652'.8--dc21

                    2002001687

**Acknowledgments**
The author and publishers are grateful to the following for permission to reproduce copyright material:
Cover photograph courtesy of NSA/Tom Pantages
Illustrations of cipher wheel, quilt squares, semaphore flags, icelandic runes and marine alphabet flags by David Westerfield; pp. 2, 11, 16, 46 Courtesy of NARA/Tom Pantages; pp. 4, 18 Summer Productions; pp. 5, 10, 24T, 24B, 30T Bettmann/Corbis; p. 8 Library of Congress/Tom Pantages; p. 9 Hulton Getty Archives; p. 17 Hulton-Deutsch Collection/Corbis; pp. 19, 20, 21T, 23T, 29 Courtesy of NSA/Tom Pantages; p. 21B Courtesy of USMC/Tom Pantages; pp. 22T, 25T The Granger Collection, NY; pp. 22B, 25B Christie's Images; p. 23C Courtesy of INSCOM/Tom Pantages; pp. 23B, 28T Tom Pantages; p. 24C Corbis; p. 26 Todd Gipstein/Corbis; p. 27 D. Mann Ding/Corbis; p. 28B Bruce Coleman, Inc.; pp. 30B, 31 Brian Warling/Heinemann Library; p. 34B Reunion des Musees Nationaux/Art Resource, NY

Every effort has been made to contact copyright holders of any material reproduced in this book. Any omissions will be rectified in subsequent printings if notice is given to the publisher.

Some words are shown in bold, **like this.** You can find out what they mean by looking in the glossary.

# Contents

# What Are Ciphers and Codes?

People have been using **ciphers** and **codes** to send secret messages for thousands of years. This book will tell you how people use ciphers and codes. You will also learn how to make your own secret messages.

Before you begin, you should know the difference between a code and a cipher. A code replaces a word, idea, or sentence with a group of letters, a word, or a **symbol.** On the other hand, in a cipher, every letter is replaced with a symbol. The symbol can be another letter, a number, or a symbol like this: $\Omega$. For example, if you give each letter of the alphabet a number (A=1, B=2, and so on), the word DOG could be written as 4–15–7.

## The Rosetta Stone

Egyptian **hieroglyphics** are one of the earliest known forms of writing. After the civilization of ancient Egypt died out, no one knew how to read hieroglyphics. Then, in 1799, a worker building a fort in Egypt discovered a stone carved with three kinds of writing. He recognized one of them as Greek, a language that is still spoken and written today. **Scholars** thought that the three kinds of writing might say the same thing. They also hoped that they could read the part that was in Greek and use this to figure out the hieroglyphics on the stone. It took a long time, but in 1822, a man named Jean-François Champollion finally figured out the hieroglyphics. The stone, known as the Rosetta Stone, is now in the British Museum in London, England.

Messages can be put into codes (**encoded**) or into ciphers (**enciphered**) by a person called a **cryptographer.** The messages can then be figured out—**decoded** or **deciphered**—by a person called a **cryptanalyst.** Together, the process of making codes and ciphers, **cryptography,** and the study of breaking them, **cryptanalysis,** are known as **cryptology.**

We can't be sure when the first cipher or code was written. However, **historians** do know that around the year 1900 B.C.E. in Egypt, a man chiseled, or cut, some strange symbols onto a tomb. Instead of using the usual hieroglyphics known to his countrymen, he changed them a little bit. Historians think he did this on purpose. This is the earliest example that we know of today of someone changing his or her system of writing.

Many ancient cultures used codes and ciphers to send secret messages. The Roman ruler Julius Caesar, who lived from 100 B.C.E. to 44 B.C.E., invented a simple secret cipher. Alexander the Great, a king of Macedonia who lived from 356 B.C.E. to 323 B.C.E., also used a secret code. He had secret messages put on the wooden pole at the center of a **scroll** instead of writing them on the scroll itself. The native peoples of Australia, called Aborigines, and Native Americans used smoke signals as a kind of code.

Julius Caesar was a great Roman general and **statesman** who helped to make Rome a vast empire.

# Cryptology and the Arabs

The ancient Arabs were fascinated by words, and they loved to tell stories. They also loved riddles, puns, **rebuses,** and other word games, including secret writing. As early as 855 C.E., they used **substitution** alphabets.

Their culture was different from those before it in a special way—the Arabs were the first to develop the science of **cryptanalysis.** Before that, people wrote in **ciphers,** but no one had studied how to **decipher** the messages without a **key.**

In 1412, an Arab author named Qalqashandi wrote a fourteen-volume encyclopedia that included a large section on **cryptography.** Qalqashandi knew that there were many ways to **encode** or **encipher** messages: one letter could replace another, a word could be written backward, every other word could be written backward, letters could be replaced with numbers, one letter could be replaced with two letters or numbers, one word could substitute for another, and pictures could represent words or ideas.

## A Transposition Cipher: The Rail Fence

In a **transposition cipher,** the letters of the **plaintext**—the original message that will be enciphered—are mixed up in some way. One technique that does this is the rail fence system.

To start this cipher, write the words of your message—LOOK WHAT WE DID—on two lines. The first letter goes on the first line, the second letter goes on the second line, the third letter goes back on the first line, and so on, going back and forth between letters and lines.

**L O W A W D D**

**O K H T E I**

But there's more: the total number of letters should be a multiple of four, such as 8, 12, 16, or 20. If it is not a multiple of four, extra letters should be added until it is. These meaningless letters are called **nulls.** Here, we added three nulls—X, Q, and P—to the end to make a multiple of four.

# L O W A W D D Q
## O K H T E I X P

Once the total number of letters is a multiple of four, write down the letters in the first row. Then write down the letters in the second row, putting both rows on one line.

## L O W A W D D Q O K H T E I X P

Now divide the letters into groups of four. This is the enciphered message.

## L O W A   W D D Q   O K H T   E I X P

To decipher a message written this way, first divide the text exactly in half by drawing a line through it.

## L O W A   W D D Q | O K H T   E I X P

You can read the message by looking at the first letter of the first half, the first letter of the second half, the second letter of the first half, the second letter of the second half, and so on. Don't confuse yourself by reading the nulls at the end. They are there only to confuse the "enemy"!

## L O O K   W H A T   W E   D I D

The secret message was divided into groups of four to make it hard for someone to figure out where the words begin and end. In a cipher, text is often divided into groups of four or groups of five, with nulls to fill in whenever necessary.

# Cryptology in the American Revolutionary War

George Washington, our nation's first president, depended on **cryptanalysts** to discover British war secrets.

This photo shows part of Benjamin Church's enciphered letter to General Gage. Cryptanalysts broke the **code.**

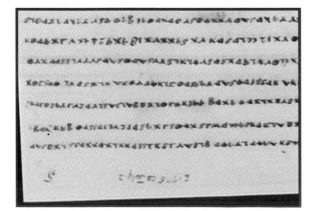

During the American Revolutionary War (1775–1783), **enciphered** messages were often used. One such message made its way to George Washington, who was commander of the Continental army. The woman who sent the letter had asked her friend Godfrey Wenwood to deliver it to some British officers. But Wenwood was a Patriot, in favor of American independence from Britain. He was curious about the letter, so he and a friend broke its seal. It was written in a **cipher** of many different **symbols**, and they could not figure it out.

A short time later, the woman sent a note to Wenwood asking why her first letter had not been delivered. This made him more suspicious. He spoke to Washington, who could not break the cipher either. Washington had the woman brought to his office and demanded to know what the letter said. She finally admitted that it was from her boyfriend, Benjamin Church Jr. Washington was surprised that Church—the director of hospitals and a member of the Sons of Liberty, a Patriot group—would be sending letters to the British army.

Church insisted that the letter was really for his brother and that it contained no secrets, but someone was finally found who could break the cipher. In the letter, Church told British general Thomas Gage many secrets about the Continental army, such as where the army was and what it was planning to do next.

Washington sent Church to prison. When his prison term ended, he was sent to the West Indies and told never to return to the United States. Mysteriously, his ship never arrived in the West Indies. No one knows what happened to him.

Near the end of the war, a man named Benedict Arnold was in charge of the Patriot **military** base in West Point, New York. But he was secretly working with a young British major, John André, to surrender West Point to the British.

Benedict Arnold was once a well-respected Continental army officer. However, his dealings with the British turned Americans against him, and he was known as a **traitor.** He spent his last days in England.

The two men used a book code to communicate. Any book can be used in this type of code as long as the sender and the receiver both have a copy. Each word in the message of a book code is represented by three different numbers: the first stands for the page on which the word is found, the second stands for the line, and the third stands for the word. Periods are placed between each number. For example, if the word to be used was on page 55, in the eighth line, and was the third word, the code for that word would be 55.8.3.

The entire plan was stopped when André was captured and hanged. Arnold managed to escape to England.

## Know It

**Cryptography** is commonly used during wartime. For thousands of years, opposing sides in wars have tried to pass messages in special codes or ciphers so the enemy cannot read them.

# Cryptology in the American Civil War

The telegraph used bursts of electricity to send messages over a wire. The operator broke the flow of electricity along a wire by tapping on a lever that used short and longer bursts of electricity, with space in between the bursts. The short and long bursts represented letters.

| | | | | | |
|---|---|---|---|---|---|
| A | •— | N | —• | 0 | —————— |
| B | —••• | O | ——— | 1 | •———— |
| C | —•—• | P | •——• | 2 | ••——— |
| D | —•• | Q | ——•— | 3 | •••—— |
| E | • | R | •—• | 4 | ••••— |
| F | ••—• | S | ••• | 5 | ••••• |
| G | ——• | T | — | 6 | —•••• |
| H | •••• | U | ••— | 7 | ——••• |
| I | •• | V | •••— | 8 | ———•• |
| J | •——— | W | •—— | 9 | ————• |
| K | —•— | X | —••— | • | •—•—•— |
| L | •—•• | Y | —•—— | , | ——••—— |
| M | —— | Z | ——•• | ? | ••——•• |

**Cryptology** was also used during the American Civil War (1861–1865). The Union and Confederate armies put letters into **codes** or **ciphers** so that the enemy would not be able to read the messages if they **intercepted** them.

The most popular cipher used during the Civil War was one that involved the **telegraph, patented** in 1837 by an American man named Samuel F. B. Morse. The telegraph could send messages over a wire, similar to the way our telephone and e-mail messages are sent today. **Telegraphers** used a code of long and short sounds, called Morse code, to send messages. A written dot stands for a short sound, and a dash stands for a long one.

General McClellan of the Union army asked a telegrapher named Anson Stager to develop a new cipher using the telegraph. Stager created a cipher that was soon being used by many in the Union forces. Stager's cipher used **transposition, nulls,** and other more complicated methods to **encrypt**

Morse code uses a series of dots and dashes to represent letters and numbers.

messages. Sometimes, names of important places and people were replaced with other words. For example, in one **telegram** the city of Richmond, Virginia, was called NEPTUNE and the city of Vicksburg, Mississippi, was called ODOR. President Lincoln spent many hours in the War Department telegraph office reading incoming and outgoing messages so he could keep up with what was going on.

The Confederate army also used cryptology, but instead of having one cipher, each commanding officer chose his own. This made it difficult for officers to communicate with each other. Sometimes errors occurred as the messages were **enciphered,** so that even using the right **key** would not help to figure out the messages. Still, the Union army was often able to **decipher** the Confederate messages that they intercepted.

The Confederates were not able to decipher many of the messages they intercepted from the Union army. Sometimes they even published the letters in local newspapers, asking if the readers could figure out what the messages said!

## A hairy scheme

During the Civil War, a woman named Rose Greenhow was a spy for the Confederacy. When she found out that the Union army was coming, she asked her friend Betty Duvall to carry a message to the Confederates. Rose wrote the message on a piece of paper and folded it up very small and sewed it together. Next, Betty put her long hair up into a bun. Rose stuck the note into Betty's bun, then pushed a comb into her hair to make sure the package didn't fall out. Rose and Betty's plan was successful—the Confederates were warned.

# Quilt Codes and Spirituals Show the Way to Freedom

In the 1800s, **abolitionists** in the United States and in Canada formed a plan to help slaves escape to freedom. They called their system the Underground Railroad. This "railroad" was made up of people who lived in different parts of the country and who helped the slaves by giving them food, shelter, clothing, and helpful information. Usually the slaves traveled by night and hid during the day. They often went all the way to Canada, because if they stayed in the United States they could be captured and forced back into slavery.

Slaves were not allowed to learn to read and write, so they made up special **codes** and signals to use to help one another escape. They would sometimes even use these codes in front of their owners.

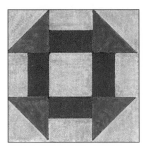

This pattern is called Monkey Wrench. It signaled to the slave to get his or her tools together and prepare to escape.

This pattern is the Wagon Wheel. It signaled to the slave that it was time to put his or her things into the wagon.

The Crossroads pattern signaled that the slave was to meet someone at Cleveland, Ohio. Cleveland is where slaves would go to take a ferry across Lake Erie to Canada.

This pattern is called Tumbling Boxes, or Tumbling Blocks. It meant it was time to escape.

One kind of code that some people think the slaves used is called a quilt code. Certain quilt patterns had special meaning to slaves and others on the Underground Railroad. The quilts were hung over fences in the slave quarters, where the slaves lived on **plantations.** No one became suspicious of this, because people often aired out their quilts by hanging them on fences this way.

An abolitionist named Alexander Ross also made up a word code to help slaves get through the Underground Railroad in secret. He talked about having to carry some "packages"—male slaves were called "hardware" and female slaves were "dry goods." His code used numbers for some locations and words for others. For example, Pennsylvania was called "Ten." Detroit, Michigan, was "Midnight." Cleveland, Ohio, was "Hope."

Another way that African-American slaves could secretly communicate was through folk songs called spirituals. Slaves sang spirituals while working in the plantation fields and also at secret church meetings. Many spirituals tell stories from the Bible, but the lyrics were often a special code that held hidden meanings, too. For example, a spiritual called "Wade in the Water" told an escaping slave to go into the river so the dogs used to track him would lose his scent.

Harriet Tubman, an escaped slave who guided more than 300 slaves to freedom on the Underground Railroad, used spirituals to send messages to others on the Underground Railroad. Tubman sang the spiritual "Go Down, Moses" to the slaves she led. Slaves identified with the Bible story of Moses, who led his people to freedom just like Tubman did. In this song, "Moses" stood for Harriet Tubman and "Pharaoh" meant slave owner. Slaves could even sing this song in front of their owners, who didn't recognize the hidden meaning in the song.

# Semaphore Signaling

Before the **telegraph** was invented, people used other ways of signaling to communicate with one another. Some systems used visual signals, because you can see farther than you can hear. For example, when sailors on a ship wanted to send a message to another ship or to someone on shore, a signaler on the ship would put the message into **code** using flags. A man would stand on the deck of the ship and hold a small flag in each hand. He would hold his arms in different positions to indicate letters or other messages. This kind of code is called **semaphore.**

Semaphore signaling was also used to send messages on land. Signalers stood on high towers and signaled with flags, and receivers would look through **telescopes** to see the messages. Semaphore signals were also used on railroads to communicate with passing trains or people at train stations. This kind of signaling on railroads is still used sometimes, but instead of using people with flags, a post with a movable "arm" at the top is used. Train engineers know how to read the signals given by the arm's different positions.

The signals used in semaphore are shown on the next page. Semaphore movements are a lot like the movements of the hands of a clock. Look closely at the pictures and you will notice that the signals start with the left arm straight down and the right arm moved just to the right of the body. One flag stays straight down while the other moves to different positions around the body. When that flag completes the circle around the body with the letter *G,* another cycle begins. In this cycle, the other flag also moves.

## Smoke signals

Native Americans sometimes used smoke signals as codes. Smoke signalers built fires on hilltops. They could send only short messages by smoke signals—messages signaling danger, for example, or telling the direction that a herd of animals was traveling. Two columns of smoke supposedly signaled that a war party had returned successfully. Aborigines, the native people of Australia, also used smoke signals.

Semaphore flags that were used for signaling between two ships were usually red and yellow. Flags used to signal between a ship and land were red and white.

# World War I

World War I was fought around the world from 1914 until 1918. Germany, Italy, Austria-Hungary, and other countries fought on one side, while Russia, Great Britain, France, and the United States—called the Allied Forces—fought on the other side.

On August 5, 1914, sailors from the British ship *Telconia* pulled up Germany's **telegraph** cables from the floor of the North Sea, cut them, and dropped them back into the water. This forced Germany to send all its messages by radio, over signals that other countries could also listen to. Germany's secret messages were then **intercepted** by its enemies. But once they had them, these countries still had to break the **codes** and **ciphers**.

The four- and five-letter groupings of numbers can be clearly seen in this photo of the Zimmermann telegram.

## The Zimmermann telegram

Alfred Zimmermann was the German secretary of foreign affairs during World War I. On January 16, 1917, he sent a **telegram** to the German minister in Mexico. The telegram was **encrypted** in a series of four- and five-letter groupings of numbers that stood for words. British **cryptanalysts** intercepted and **decrypted** the telegram but did not present it to U.S. President Woodrow Wilson until February 24. Wilson released the telegram to the press, who published it on March 1. While most Americans had been against entering the war, many of them changed their minds after they read the telegram. The telegram stated that if Mexico would join Germany in the war, Germany would give Mexico the "lost territory in Texas, New Mexico, and Arizona" when the war was won. The people of the United States did not want this to happen, so they began to support the country's entry into the war to fight Germany.

This World War I soldier is using a **heliograph** to send a secret message. A heliograph used mirrors to send messages in Morse code by reflecting the light of the sun.

Britain asked Sir Alfred Ewing to try to decrypt many of the messages. First, he went to the library and studied everything he could find about ciphers and codes. Then he called some professor friends, and they tried to decrypt the messages. But they could not do it. Then one day, a German ship wrecked off the coast of Russia. In the wreckage, the Russians discovered some German **code books,** and they delivered them to the British, hoping that they could use them to break the German codes. At first, the British cryptanalysts could not find the **key** to the cipher in the books. Finally, though, they figured it out. A few months later, more code books were found in another shipwreck. Soon the cryptanalysts had found out how to decrypt radio codes as well.

The Germans did not know that the British could now read their messages, so they kept using the same codes. The British continued to intercept and decrypt the messages. They recovered more code books from sunken ships, so they were able to discover more and more of the keys and **key words** the Germans used. By the end of the war, it is estimated that the British cryptographers had intercepted and deciphered about 15,000 German secret messages.

# World War II

In the years after World War I, machines were invented that could put messages into **codes** and **ciphers**. In 1939, another war broke out, known as World War II. Germany, Italy, and Japan fought on one side of the war, and Great Britain, the United States, and the Soviet Union—as well as many other countries—fought on the other side.

During World War II, many messages were **encrypted** by machines. One machine the Germans used was called Enigma. There were several different versions of this machine, each more complicated than the last.

The first Enigma machine was invented by a German man named Arthur Scherbius in 1918. This machine uses a complicated system of wheels that change a message into a **substitution cipher.** It has a keyboard with the 26 letters of the alphabet, similar to a computer keyboard. The machine operator chooses three wheels from a selection of five to eight wheels, and puts them into slots inside the machine. As the operator types the message, the wheels move, changing the letters that are being typed into the machine. For example, if the operator typed "The plane leaves at midnight," the

This is a photo of an Enigma machine. This machine helped the Germans encrypt thousands of messages during World War II.

turning wheels would create an unreadable string of letters instead. All together, there are more than 17,000 ways a message can be written on the Enigma machine!

People trying to **decipher** the message can do so only if they know which three wheels were put into the machine, and the order they were placed in the machine. In addition, the machine has other ways to encrypt messages besides the wheels. The Enigma also contains 26 wires connected to the keyboard that can scramble up the letters.

Because the Enigma machine was so complicated, it took Germany's enemies a long time to figure out how it worked. By 1938, though, the Polish secret service was able to interpret about three of every four messages the Germans typed on the Enigma. In 1939, the Poles shared what they had learned with the British and French, so even more of the Enigma messages the Germans created were deciphered.

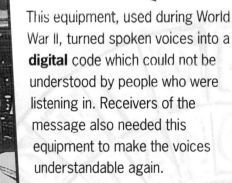

This equipment, used during World War II, turned spoken voices into a **digital** code which could not be understood by people who were listening in. Receivers of the message also needed this equipment to make the voices understandable again.

# Navajo Code Talkers

During much of World War II, the U.S. Marines were fighting the Japanese in the Pacific Ocean. They needed to send many messages by radio, but they also knew that the Japanese were listening to their radio conversations. The Japanese were good at breaking **codes**, so the Marines were looking for a code no one could break. In 1942, a man named Philip Johnston came to Major General Clayton B. Vogel, the head of the **Amphibious Corps,** Pacific Fleet. He suggested that the Navajo language would be a good code. Johnston grew up on a Navajo reservation and spoke the language. He explained that the language is only spoken—never written—and is very difficult to learn and understand. Only those who have been around Navajo speakers for a long time can understand the different tones of voice and the way that words are arranged in a sentence.

Johnston proved that Navajo speakers could **encode, transmit,** and **decode** messages faster than the **cipher** machines that the **military** was using at that time. Then the military did a study to find out how many non-Navajo people could speak the Navajo language. They found only 28 people other than Navajos who knew how to speak it, and none of those persons was German or Japanese.

These two Navajo code talkers, part of a U.S. Marine unit, are relaying messages over a field radio somewhere in the Pacific during World War II.

Vogel decided that the Navajo language was a good code. Two hundred Navajos signed up to help, and they made a code and wrote a dictionary for it.

The code talkers went to work. During one big battle at Iwo Jima, an island in the Pacific Ocean, six Navajo men sent and received more than 800 messages in two days. By the end of the war, the Marines had hired 420 code talkers.

The code worked in two main ways. For words that were used often, the code talkers used close Navajo words from a prepared list. Other words had to be spelled out. The sender would speak several Navajo words. The person who received the message knew to translate the words into English, then write down the first letter of the English word. For example, if the code talker said the word *lin* (Navajo for "horse"), the decoder knew to write down an *H*. This continued until the entire message was spelled out.

The code was used for every military assault in the Pacific from 1942 to 1945. The Japanese were never able to break the Navajo code. The code worked so well that the military continued to use it long after the war ended.

In 1992, former Navajo code talkers were honored for their wartime efforts by the U.S. government. Because no one could break the Navajo code, the U.S. government thought it might still be valuable as code even after the war ended. For that reason, the code talkers received recognition only recently.

# Famous Cryptologists

## Sir Francis Walsingham

Elizabeth I was England's queen in 1586, but her cousin, Mary, Queen of Scots, thought that the throne should belong to her. Mary was in prison in England, but with the help of her supporters she planned to take the throne from Elizabeth and become queen herself.

One of the chief plotters, Anthony Babington, smuggled **enciphered** letters to Mary in beer barrels. But a busy intelligence agency headed by Elizabeth's friend Sir Francis Walsingham soon grew aware of the letters. Walsingham's spies **intercepted** the letters and **deciphered** them. He soon began to understand what Mary was planning, so he kept all the letters, hoping that in one of them Mary would reveal her part in the plot. She finally did, but Walsingham also wanted to know who else was involved. To find out, he added a paragraph to a letter sent by Mary, written in the same **cipher** the letter was in. In the paragraph, Walsingham—pretending to be Mary—asked the **conspirator** to name the six men who would carry out the plan. All the conspirators—including Mary—were caught and put to death.

Sir Francis Walsingham built up England's secret intelligence agency.

With the help of Walsingham, Elizabeth I (shown here) kept Mary, Queen of Scots, from becoming Queen of England.

# Herbert Yardley

Yardley was an American **cryptologist** during World War I. When the United States entered the war in 1917, Yardley was put in charge of a special American **cryptology bureau** called MI-8. It took only a few months for MI-8 to break most of Germany's **codes**. After the war, Yardley wrote a book, *The American Black Chamber,* about his adventures as a cryptologist. He ended up working in intelligence departments in China and Canada. He is often called the father of modern American cryptology.

This picture of Herbert Yardley was taken in the early 1930s.

The Purple Analog used electrical impulses and a scrambled alphabet. With this machine, a letter could be represented by more than one ciphered letter. For example, in one place, a *P* could be an *L*, but the next time it was typed in the same message, it might be a *J*.

# William F. Friedman

Friedman was well known in the world of cryptology for his great skill at reconstructing cipher machines. During World War II, Friedman became the chief **cryptanalyst** for the War Department. In 1941, he and his staff deciphered a secret code used by the Japanese. Friedman built what he called the Purple Analog, named after the kind of cipher the Japanese used. His machine looked and worked a lot like the original Japanese version. Using his Purple machine on the evening of December 6, 1941, Friedman discovered that Pearl Harbor was to be attacked the next morning. By the time the message reached Washington, though, it was too late, and Pearl Harbor was not warned. After the war, Friedman continued his work at the Department of Defense.

William Friedman is shown here in the late 1950s. He was the first person to show how mathematics and cryptology could work together.

# Cryptology in Literature

Edgar Allan Poe wrote a story about a cipher.

Many authors have been fascinated by **cryptology.** Edgar Allan Poe, who wrote scary stories in the 1800s, wrote one called *The Gold Bug.* This story is about an **enciphered** message written in invisible ink. Once it is revealed, the **cipher** tells where a pirate's treasure is buried.

Charles Dickens is another author who used secret **codes** in one of his works. In *A Tale of Two Cities* (about the French Revolution, which took place from 1789 to 1799), one of the characters, Madame Defarge, spends much of her time knitting. It is only near the end of the book that the reader discovers that she was knitting secret coded messages into her yarn!

One of Charles Dickens's characters used a secret code to send messages.

It probably isn't surprising that Sir Arthur Conan Doyle, the author of the Sherlock Holmes stories, was fascinated by cryptology. In one story called "The Adventure of the Dancing Men," Holmes solves a mystery by **deciphering** a strange cipher written in **characters** that look like dancing men.

The best way to make sure no one can read what you write in your diary is to use a secret cipher or code! Many people throughout history have done this. One man

Arthur Conan Doyle wrote many detective stories, including one about a secret code.

who wrote his diary in cipher is Samuel Pepys, pronounced "Peeps." He lived in England and wrote his diary from 1660 to 1669. The diary took up more than 3,000 pages by the time he stopped writing it. Pepys didn't write the diary in regular English, but in a special kind of writing called **tachygraphy.** Few people knew how to decipher this kind of writing, and for many years after he died, Pepys's diaries were kept in a library but were not **translated.** Finally, after three years of work, a man named John Smith finished translating the diaries in 1822. The diary was first published in 1825, and it is still being published and sold in bookstores today.

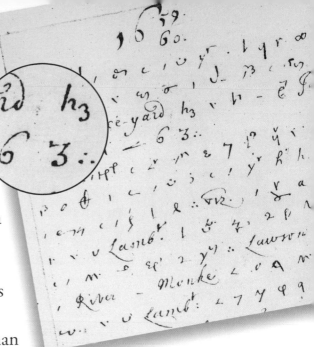

This page is from the diary of Samuel Pepys. It is written in a kind of shorthand that was not widely known in Pepys's time and is almost never seen today.

## Ciphers in war

Throughout history, people have used ciphers when writing letters to friends, and when writing letters for more important reasons, such as spying or passing on secrets. The story of Marie Antoinette and her husband, Louis XIV, King of France, is one example of the use of ciphers. Louis and Marie had lots of money and fine food, while the people of France became poorer and hungrier. The citizens thought their king and queen did nothing to help the poor, and they planned a revolution. Starting in 1783, Marie wrote letters in cipher to her friend Count Axel Fersen. Some of the letters dealt with their plans to escape. In 1791, Fersen helped Louis and Marie get away from the people who were planning the revolution. But the king and queen were caught as they tried to escape, and they were put in prison. In 1793, both Louis and Marie Antoinette were put to death by **guillotine.**

# Modern Cryptology

Today, **cryptology** is more complicated than ever. Computers play an important role in modern cryptology. Computer programmers know many languages that are impossible to understand unless you have been specially trained. They are not **ciphers** in the same way the other examples in this book are, because they are not "secret"—they just have to be learned.

## Binary code

One very basic computer language is called **binary code.** This language is made up entirely of zeroes and ones. Each zero or one is called a **bit.** A binary number could look like this: 10011010.

## Programming languages

Programmers use computer languages to program computers. These are not languages that are spoken by people, but computers know how to read these languages and know what to do when they read them.

# A career in cryptology

If you are interested in cryptology, you may want to think about becoming a **cryptanalyst** or **cryptographer** someday. Modern cryptologists need skills in mathematics, computer programming, engineering, and languages. They also need to use their creativity to solve problems. People who are cryptologists need to be able to concentrate for long periods of time on one thing, and they should like to solve problems, even those that seem impossible to solve at first. Modern cryptographers helped think of ways to **encode** a person's credit card information while it is being scanned.

Computers and programmers use binary code to represent numbers, letters, and other **characters.** Only zeroes and ones are used in binary code.

## Public key cryptography

In the 1970s, public key **cryptography** became known. In this system, just as in the ciphers in this book, a **key** is used to send messages—and that same key can be known to the public. But even with a known key, the message can't be **deciphered,** because there is still another secret key. The **code book** is in two parts, and even if one key is known, the other key is still secret, so the message cannot be deciphered.

## Jobs for cryptologists

The National Security Agency is a large government agency that hires many cryptanalysts and cryptographers. They will hire people from different academic backgrounds. Their main concern is that their employees are good at solving problems and like to work hard.

Other kinds of jobs for people who enjoy cryptology are found in a field called information systems. The work involves using cryptologic technology to make sure that computer files are safe and secure for people and businesses. Cryptologists also make sure that when people use credit cards to buy things over the Internet, their personal information and credit card numbers are kept safe. A person who is interested in this kind of job should study mathematics and computer science. It's never too early to start preparing for your future!

# The Tools of Cryptology

Cryptographers have used many different tools to make **ciphers** and **codes**. The most basic tools are a pencil or pen and paper. Many cryptographers use **graph paper** because the layout of squares helps them line up **characters** with other characters or **symbols**. This works especially well for creating **substitution ciphers,** when one letter stands for another.

Another simple method of creating ciphers is to use a Saint-Cyr slide. It has two parts: a strip of paper or cardboard with the alphabet written on it, and a longer, narrower strip with the alphabet written on it twice in a row. There are two small slits below the alphabet in the larger piece or paper. The narrow strip is slotted through them. Sliding the narrow strip from side to side will line its alphabet up with different letters under the large piece's alphabet, creating a cipher. You can make a Saint-Cyr slide yourself. Just make sure that you space the letters evenly, so the letters in the two strips' alphabets will line up exactly above one another.

## The amazing brain

Do you know what this is? It's the most important tool in **cryptology**—the brain! Not only do **cryptographers** and **cryptanalysts** need to think hard when they are working, but they often need to carry around **keys** in their memories so no one else can figure out the code!

A cipher **disk** is flat and is made of at least two disks. One disk shows the letters of the alphabet. The second disk can also have letters, or it can have numbers or other symbols. The person making the cipher turns the disk and lines up a letter and symbol. Leaving the disk in that position, he or she then writes the message by seeing which letter lines up with which character.

A cipher wheel like this one was invented by Thomas Jefferson. The cipher wheel consists of 36 wooden wheels, marked with the alphabet and mounted on a pole. The **encoder** turns each wheel until he or she has a 36-letter message, then turns the entire **cylinder** and writes down any **horizontal** line of text. The **decoder** turns the wheel to find the written line, then studies the wheel until he or she sees a line that makes sense. That line is the message.

The United States used the SIGABA machine for important communications during World War II. It was the only machine system that was never broken by an enemy.

# Invisible Ink

People don't always write secret messages in **ciphers** or **codes**. Sometimes they use what is called **steganography**. This means that no one can see the message at all!

Writing a message in invisible ink is one kind of steganography. Invisible ink has been around for thousands of years. You can make your own invisible ink from things you have around your home or that you can buy from a grocery store.

You can write an invisible ink message between the lines of a regular letter. Write a short note in regular ink, making sure to leave enough room between the lines for your invisible message.

You can read the secret letter written between the lines of the regular letter if you look closely. The secret letter was written with invisible ink.

## Your own invisible ink

You can make invisible ink out of lemon or lime juice. You will need a fresh lemon or lime, a cotton swab, and an index card or notebook paper. Have an adult helper squeeze some juice from the fruit. Then dip the cotton swab into the juice and write a message onto the index card or notebook paper. Let the "ink" dry. The receiver should ask an adult to heat the paper with an iron on a low setting. It will take a few minutes before the "ink" becomes visible.

Here are the tools you will need to write your own secret messages with invisible ink.

To make sure your cotton swab stays wet, you may need to dip it into the "ink" a few times while writing your message.

Another way to make invisible ink is with baking soda and water. Mix one teaspoon of baking soda into two teaspoons of water. Make sure you stir it well so the baking soda dissolves. With a cotton swab, write your message onto an index card or piece of notebook paper. When the "ink" dries, give the message to a friend and tell the friend to paint the card or paper with grape juice concentrate, a product that can be found in the frozen juice section of a grocery store. The message will magically appear! You should wear old clothes or a smock when using the grape juice concentrate, though, because it can stain your clothes.

Always ask an adult to use the iron for you. Be sure to tell your adult helper not to let the iron sit on the paper for more than a second, or the paper will burn!

The last way to write an invisible message is to use white or off-white wax. A birthday candle works well for this. With the candle, write a message on a piece of white paper. You may have to cut the wick of the candle off to do this. To reveal the message, rub over the paper lightly with a dark-colored crayon. Don't color too hard, or the message won't show up. You can also use a white crayon to write a secret message—just remember to rub the darker colored crayon lightly over the message.

# Ancient Ciphers

The ancient Roman ruler Julius Caesar is said to have developed a **cipher.** In this cipher, each letter of the alphabet is replaced by another letter. This kind of cipher is called a **substitution cipher,** because one letter is **substituted** for another.

Caesar ciphers are fairly simple. First, write down all the letters of the alphabet. Then choose a **key** number. We will use the number 5. Put your pencil on *A,* then move it five letters to the right. You will land on *F.* That's where your substitution alphabet will start. Write an *A* below the letter *F* in your first alphabet, a *B* below the letter *G,* and continue writing the regular alphabet. When you get to *Z* you will still have letters left over. Go back to the beginning and continue writing them. If you do it correctly, *Z* will be written under the letter *E.*

| A | B | C | D | E | F | G | H | I | J | K | L | M | N | O | P | Q | R | S | T | U | V | W | X | Y | Z |
|---|---|---|---|---|---|---|---|---|---|---|---|---|---|---|---|---|---|---|---|---|---|---|---|---|---|
| V | W | X | Y | Z | A | B | C | D | E | F | G | H | I | J | K | L | M | N | O | P | Q | R | S | T | U |

Every letter in the message gets replaced with the letter written below it. With the substitution alphabet above, the word HELLO is written CZGGJ. But don't use apostrophes in the words in your ciphers—including them will help the enemy break your **code!**

See if you can **decipher** these messages using the above alphabet (answers on page 47):

## XVI TJP MZVY OCDN?  CDYZ OCZ FZT!

For a different kind of Caesar cipher, use shifted numbers instead of letters. For example, start with the number 4, and place it under the letter *A.* Then continue writing the rest of the numbers until you get to the end of the alphabet. Or you can start the Caesar cipher at *Z* instead of *A.*

Another ancient cipher is the Polybius **grid,** developed by an ancient Greek named Polybius. It is sometimes also called a Greek square. The square is divided into a grid, or a group of smaller squares of equal size. The Polybius grid is made up of 25 smaller squares.

Because there are 25 squares in the grid but 26 letters in the English alphabet, one of the letters should either be left out or doubled up with another letter. The pair "YZ" is often doubled up because they are not used often. The **cryptanalyst** can use the other letters of the message to tell which of these two letters is the one that fits in a certain word.

| # | 1 | 2 | 3 | 4 | 5 |
|---|---|---|---|---|---|
| 1 | a | b | c | d | e |
| 2 | f | g | h | i | j |
| 3 | k | l | m | n | o |
| 4 | p | q | r | s | t |
| 5 | u | v | w | x | yz |

A Polybius grid has 25 squares, in rows going across and columns going up and down. Each row and column is numbered, and a letter is placed in each square. The row and column numbers form the cipher: the letter A is written as 11, G is 22, and M is 33.

Let's say you want to **encipher** the message MEET ME ON THE FRONT PORCH. To write this message, find the letter *M* in the grid. Next, find the row number and the column number for *M* and write down each number. Did you write 33? If so, you're right!

Now find *E*. It's in square 15. Put a hyphen between each pair of numbers. Continue until you have enciphered the entire message. When you are finished, you should have this:

33 15 15 45 33 15 35 34 45 23 15 21 43 35 34 45 41 35 43 13 23
M  E  E  T  M  E  O  N  T  H  E  F  R  O  N  T  P  O  R  C  H

You could put spaces between the words, but that would make it easier for someone to **decipher** the message. To make the grid harder to decipher, you could mix up the letters on the outside of the grid by putting them in a different order.

When you send a ciphered or coded message to someone, you need to make sure he or she will be able to decipher or **decode** the message. To do this, the receiver will need a key. The key tells the receiver how to decipher or decode the message. The person who receives the message above would need to know that you used a Polybius grid. He or she would also need to know how the columns and rows were labeled. Then that person could decipher the message using the grid.

# Pigpen Cipher

Over time, **cryptographers** have developed **ciphers** and **codes** that were more and more complicated. One of these is called the pigpen cipher. It is drawn in a special pattern of lines, this time using 26 sections.

To include all the letters in the English alphabet, you would need to draw two tic-tac-toe patterns and two patterns in the shape of large Xs. A dot goes in each section of the second pattern of each kind.

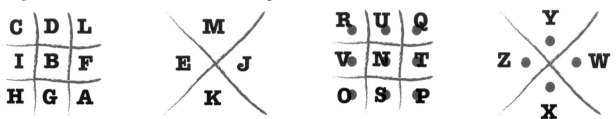

Now put one letter of the alphabet in each compartment. You can put any letter anywhere you like. Just remember to keep a copy of the **key** so you and your friends will know how to **encipher** and **decipher** messages.

To write the cipher, draw the section without the letter. For example, instead of **B**, draw ⊔. For **M**, draw ∨, and so on. The message CANNOT MEET AFTER SCHOOL will look like this:

⌐⌐⌐⊡⊡⊡·⌐⊡   ∨⟩⟩⊡   ⌐⌐⊡⟩⌐   ⌐⌐⌐⌐⌐⌐

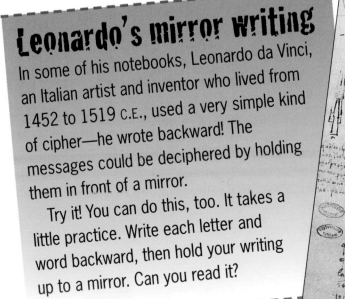

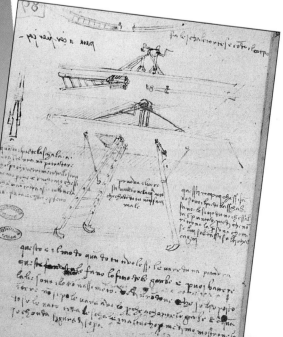

Here's another example of a pigpen cipher. Can you figure it out (answer on page 47)?

⊔⊐⊔  ⌄⊓⊔  ⌐⌐⌐⌐  ⊏⊐⟩  ⊏⟩⌐⊏

# Runes

Special **characters** that were used to write from the third century to the seventeenth century in Britain, Scandinavia, Iceland, and Northern Europe are called runes. These runes were put together in their own alphabet. Many **scholars** think that the **characters** of the runic alphabet came from an ancient Etruscan alphabet of Northern Italy. You could write a message using runes instead of the regular alphabet, but anyone who was familiar with runes would be able to read the message.

**Know It**

Like many other ancient alphabets, runes were written and read from right to left.

# Icelandic Runes

| Letter | Pronunciation | Rune |
|---|---|---|
| A | . . . . .Like the A in aha! | ↑↗ |
| B | | ᛒ |
| C | | ᛘ |
| D | | ↑↑↑↑ |
| E | . . . . .Like the e in men | ϕ |
| F | | ᚠᚠ |
| G | | ᚠᚠᚠ |
| H | | ✳ |
| I | . . . . .Like the i in simple | ᛁᛚ |
| J | | |
| K | | ᚠᛉ |
| L | | ⌈ |
| M | | ᛉᛉ |
| N | | ᛌ |

| Letter | Pronunciation | Rune |
|---|---|---|
| O | Like the o in song | ↑ |
| P | | ᛘᛘ |
| Q | | ᛘᚤ |
| R | Errr as in berrrrr | ᚱᚱ |
| S | | ᛦᛦᛦᛦ |
| T | | ᛏ |
| U | Like the u in uh? | ᒐ |
| V | | |
| X | | ✕ |
| Y | Like the i in simple | ⇕ |
| Z | | |
| <THORN> | Like the th in Athens | ᚦᚦ |
| Æ/æ | Like the i in mine | ✗ |
| Öö | Like the u in murder | ᛣ |

# Key Word Cipher

A **key word cipher** is similar to a Caesar cipher, but instead of counting with a specific number, you use a key word. Say you want to send a message to your best friend. Tell your best friend the key word. Any word will work, as long as it doesn't have any repeating letters—each letter can be used only one time. We will use the word GLOW.

To create a key word cipher, write down all the letters of the alphabet. Then write the key word underneath the beginning letters of that alphabet. Now start writing the alphabet at the next letter. But don't write the letters in your key word again! Skip those letters when you come to them. Your alphabet should look like this:

| A | B | C | D | E | F | G | H | I | J | K | L | M | N | O | P | Q | R | S | T | U | V | W | X | Y | Z |
|---|---|---|---|---|---|---|---|---|---|---|---|---|---|---|---|---|---|---|---|---|---|---|---|---|---|
| G | L | O | W | A | B | C | D | E | F | H | I | J | K | M | N | P | Q | R | S | T | U | V | X | Y | Z |

As you can see, the last three letters stay the same. That's because the key word, GLOW, contains no letters past *W.* If you want, you can always use a key word that has a letter closer to the end of the alphabet. Then the last letters will be different. But leaving them the same isn't so bad. It will just confuse someone who is trying to break the cipher!

A way to make the key word cipher even harder to figure out is to change the order of the letters in the bottom row. For example, after you write the key word, fill in the rest of the alphabet letters as before, but begin with *Z* and work backward. Just make sure your friend knows how you did it!

You can also make **numerical** ciphers using a key number like an address, birthday, or telephone number, as long as the digits do not repeat.

Let's say you want to give the combination of your locker to a friend of yours, but you want to do it secretly. You can make a key number cipher. For the key number in this cipher, we'll use a birthdate: December 23. December is the twelfth month of the year. Therefore, the key number is 12–23. Write the key number at the start, and then fill in the rest of the numbers without repeating numbers already used in the key number. This example uses the numbers 0–26, but if your lock goes up to a higher number, then you will need a longer cipher.

| 0 | 1 | 2 | 3 | 4 | 5 | 6 | 7 | 8 | 9 | 10 | 11 | 12 | 13 | 14 | 15 | 16 | 17 | 18 | 19 | 20 | 21 | 22 | 23 | 24 | 25 | 26 |
|---|---|---|---|---|---|---|---|---|---|----|----|----|----|----|----|----|----|----|----|----|----|----|----|----|----|----|
| 12 | 23 | 0 | 1 | 2 | 3 | 4 | 5 | 6 | 7 | 8 | 9 | 10 | 11 | 13 | 14 | 15 | 16 | 17 | 18 | 19 | 20 | 21 | 22 | 24 | 25 | 26 |

If the real combination to your locker is 14–1–20, the combination in cipher is 13–23–19.

# Your own special cipher

A **substitution cipher** can use any kind of **symbol.** You can make up a special cipher that's yours alone and call it by your name—"the Jason cipher," for example.

Use any symbols you want to create your cipher. If you have a computer, you can find many symbols on the keyboard. But make sure you can also draw the symbols by hand so you can write them down when you can't get to your computer.

> ## Know It
> Advanced **cryptographers** sometimes use double substitutions. They first write a message using one cipher, then take the result and **encipher** it again using a different cipher. The reader needs both keys to figure it out.

The only problem with this kind of cipher is that to give someone the **key** you have to give them the entire cipher—written down. This could mean trouble if it falls into the wrong hands!

# The Twisted Path Cipher

This **transposition cipher** gets its name from the "twisted path" it uses to mix up the letters of a message. The first step is to come up with a message, such as DON'T GIVE ANN THE KEY. There are seventeen letters in this message. Do not count any punctuation, like the apostrophe in the word "don't." Punctuation gives **cryptanalysts** important clues about the message! The next step is similar to the rail fence cipher on pages 6–7: you need to add **nulls** to the message so that it is a multiple of four. Since the next closest multiple of four is twenty, you need to add three nulls:

DONT GIVE ANN THE KEY CHJ

In this cipher, *C, H,* and *J* are the nulls.

Now you need to make a **grid** that can hold all twenty letters of your message. Make one that is four squares high and five squares wide. Then put each letter of your message in a square, like this:

Next, draw a path through the grid. Below are examples of some kinds of paths you could draw. You can begin in any square: just make sure that the path goes through every square once! The **key** to this cipher is the path that you draw through the letters. Be sure to give a copy of the path you draw (without the letters) to the people who you want to be able to read the message.

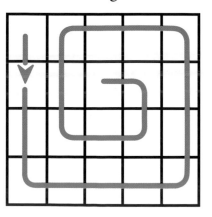

Now write down your letters in the order of the path you drew. The letters from the example on page 38—and written in groups of four—are: DINE YCHJ KNGT NOVT HEAE. This is your **enciphered** message.

To **decipher** this kind of message, you will need to draw a grid the same size as the grid used to create the message. Then, using the key, draw the correct path over the grid. Then start by putting the first letter of the enciphered message in the square where the path begins. Continue following the path, putting the second letter in the next square of the path and so on, and soon you will see the message!

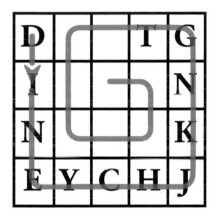

Can you figure out this twisted path cipher? Here is the key:

DUTS   THEQ   GTSA   PIDY   OSEN

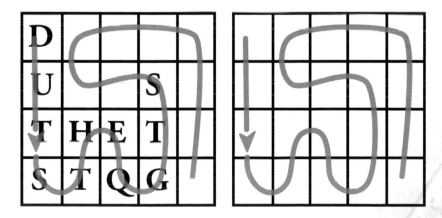

Answer on page 47.

# Break the Cipher! Some Helpful Hints

It is usually very difficult to break a **cipher** without the **key.** But if you want to try it, here are some basic tricks you should know that will often help you figure out a cipher.

First, you should find out what language the cipher is written in. Most likely, any cipher you receive will be written in English.

The English language has 26 letters. The letter used most often is *E.* Many **cryptanalysts** make a list of the most commonly used **characters** in a cipher. The list is called a **frequency** chart. They figure that the letter that shows up most frequently will be an *E.* You can test this. How many times does *E* appear in this paragraph? Then count how many times a few other letters appear, such as *P* and *M.* Which appears the most often—*E, P,* or *M?*

After *E,* the most frequently used letters are *T, O, A,* and *N.* The least frequently used letters are *V, K, Q, X, J,* and *Z.* The letter that shows up the least in the English language is *Z.* You can test this, too. Find any paragraph in this book, then count how many times you see a *Z* in that paragraph. A large percentage of the words in the English language start with one of these letters: *T, O, A, S,* or *W.* Test this. Find a sentence and see how many words start with these letters. Do you think this is true?

Another clue that cryptanalysts have is that in English, *Q* is almost always followed by a *U.* If they figure out which symbol stands for *Q,* they know the symbol after it will most likely be a *U.* Cryptanalysts look for other letter pairs, too. They call these pairs "digraphs." Some of the most commonly used letter pairs in the English language are these:

| | | | | |
|----|----|----|----|----|
| th | in | es | or | he |
| an | re | er | on | at |
| nd | st | en | of | te |
| ed | ti | hi | as | to |

Commonly used short words can often give cryptanalysts good clues for cracking a cipher. The most frequently used two-letter word in the English language is *of.* The next most frequently used word is *to,* and the third is *in.* The most frequently used three-letter words are *the* and *and.* The most frequently used four-letter word is *that.*

| from | at | had | her | I | in |
|------|------|------|------|------|------|
| have | as | was | his | he | of |
| that | is | and | you | by | on |
| with | be | are | but | or | a |
| which | it | not | for | the | to |

The list at left shows some of the most frequently used words in the English language. Because they are used so often, they are more likely to appear in a message. That means that these are good words to try first when you are trying to figure out a ciphered message.

It isn't easy to **decipher** a message if you don't have the key, but here's a challenge: ask one of your friends to put a message into a cipher. The easiest kind would be an alphabet **substitution cipher,** where your friend replaces each letter with another letter in any way he or she wishes. Then have your friend give the ciphered message to you. Using the above hints, see if you can figure out the cipher!

| a | far | in | the |
|------|------|------|------|
| and | from | is | to |
| are | had | it | was |
| as | have | not | which |
| at | he | of | with |
| be | her | on | you |
| but | his | or | |
| by | I | that | |

Most **codes** and ciphers are solved through trial and error. This means that you will probably need several tries before you solve a code or cipher. If the first words that you use don't make sense, choose something else and try that instead. Not all codes are simple—you won't always succeed on the first try—but don't give up!

# Appendix A: International Marine Signal Flags

Sailors all over the world use the same flag **code.** The system uses more than 40 flags and pennants. (A flag is either square or rectangular, while a pennant is usually shaped like a long triangle.) The flags and pennants are hoisted up a pole so that ships passing by can see them.

Ships carry **code books** that have explanations of the flags in nine languages: English, French, German, Greek, Italian, Japanese, Norwegian, Russian, and Spanish.

## International Alphabet Flags

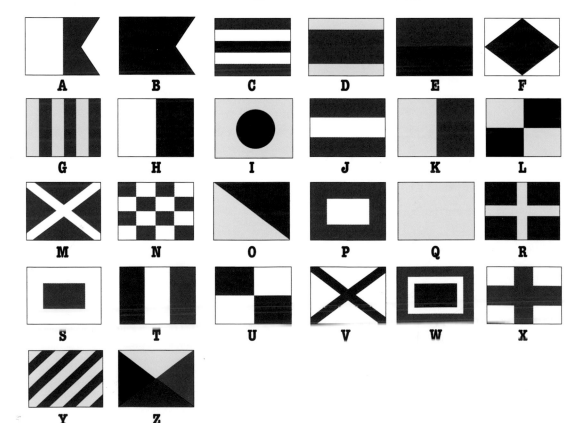

# Substitutes or Repeaters

Substitutes repeat any flag that proceeds them.

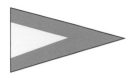 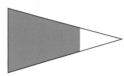

| first | second | third | fourth |

## International Numeral Pennants

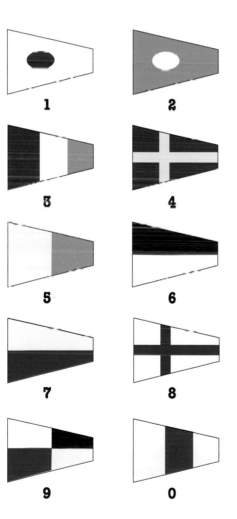

1

2

3

4

5

6

7

8

9

0

## U.S. Navy Numeral Pennants

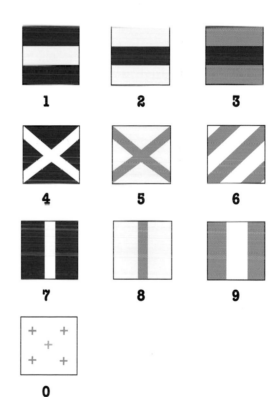

1

2

3

4

5

6

7

8

9

0

**43**

# Appendix B: Navajo Code Talkers' Dictionary

During World War II, more than 400 American Indians served as Navajo **code** talkers. They **transmitted** secret messages for the U.S. Marines, using a dictionary developed by the first code talkers. Some English words had direct **translations** in Navajo. For example, the English word "air" was translated into the Navajo word for "air." English words that did not exist in the Navajo language were translated into Navajo code words. For example, "submarine" became *besh-lo,* meaning "iron fish." You can see how the Navajo describes the way a submarine looks. The code talkers had to memorize the dictionary and the code words.

If an English word wasn't in the code talkers' dictionary, the code talker would spell out the English word letter-by-letter using Navajo words. Certain Navajo words stood for letters in the English alphabet. For example, the Navajo word *ah-tad* (girl) stood for the letter *G.* Using this technique, one way to say the word "Navy" in Navajo code would be *tsah* (needle) *wol-la-chee* (ant) *ah-keh-di-glini* (victor) *tsah-ah-dzoh* (yucca).

| ENGLISH | NAVAJO | TRANSLATION |
|---|---|---|
| air | *nilchi* | air |
| amphibious | *chal* | frog |
| armor | *besh-ye-ha-da-di-teh* | iron protector |
| captain | *besh-legai-nah-kih* | two silver bars |
| commanding officer | *hash-kay-gi-na-tah* | war chief |
| corps | *din-neh-ih* | clan |
| forward | *tehi* | let's go |
| hospital | *a-zey-al-ih* | place of medicine |
| message | *hane-al-neh* | message |
| minute | *ah-khay-el-kit-yazzie* | little hour |
| navy | *tal-kah-silago* | sea soldier |
| problem | *na-nish-tsoh* | big job |
| protect | *ah-chanh* | self defense |
| return | *na-dzah* | came back |
| sailor | *cha-le-gai* | white caps |
| succeed | *yah-tay-go-e-elah* | make good |
| surrender | *ne-na-cha* | surrender |
| truck | *chido-tso* | big auto |
| unidentified | *do-bay-hosen-e* | unidentified |
| village | *chah-ho-oh-lhan-ih* | many shelter |

# Glossary

**abolitionist** person who believes in ending slavery

**amphibious corps** group in the military that has been trained to work both on land and in the water

**binary code** code used by computers that turns every letter, word, or symbol into a series of zeroes and ones

**bit** single digit in a binary code

**bureau** specialized department or agency

**character** symbol used in writing or printing

**cipher** method of transforming a message in a way that conceals its meaning

**code** unchanging rule for replacing a letter, word, or phrase with something else

**code book** book that contains all of the keys to a country's or an organization's codes and ciphers

**conspirator** someone who joins others to secretly plot or plan something

**cryptanalysis** art and science of solving cryptograms

**cryptanalyst** person who specializes in breaking codes and ciphers

**cryptogram** message written in cipher or code

**cryptographer** person who specializes in developing codes and ciphers

**cryptography** study of enciphering or encoding messages

**cryptologist** someone who specializes in cryptology

**cryptology** science of making and breaking codes and ciphers

**cylinder** round, long object

**decipher** to put a ciphered message into plaintext

**decode** to figure out a message from a code

**decrypt** to convert something into a form that can be understood

**digital** expressed using numerical digits instead of letters or words

**disk** thin, circular object

**encipher** to put a code or message into cipher

**encode** to put a message into code

**encrypt** to encode or encipher

**frequency** number of times that something happens or shows up

**graph paper** paper that is divided into many small squares of the same size

**grid** evenly spaced lines that cross and form boxes of equal size

**guillotine** machine with a large blade used to cut people's heads off

**heliograph** machine that uses mirrors and sunlight to send messages

**hieroglyphics** system of writing made up entirely of pictures

**historian** person who specializes in the study of history

**horizontal** level with the ground; going from left to right, instead of top to bottom

**intercept** to seize or to take something that is on its way to another person and was not originally meant for you

**key** method or system used to encrypt or decrypt a message

**key word** word used to encipher a message; the same word is also used to decipher the message

**military** group formed to fight or protect, such as army or air force

**null** extra symbol with no meaning that can be inserted into a cipher

**numerical** expressed using numbers

**patent** document granted by a government that gives an inventor sole right to make, use, and sell their invention for a set period of time

**plaintext** message before it is enciphered or encoded

**plantation** very large farm common in the nineteenth century in the southern United States, usually worked by slaves

**rebus** riddle or puzzle in which words or parts of words are represented by pictures or objects

**revolution** change in political organization, sometimes as a result of a violent uprising

**scholar** someone who studies a particular field and becomes an expert

**scroll** roll of paper that can be written on, often used in ancient times

**semaphore** system of signaling using a flag in each hand

**statesman** someone involved in government or politics

**steganography** group of methods, including the use of invisible ink, for hiding an entire message within another

**substitute** replacing one thing with another, usually similar thing

**substitution cipher** cipher in which one letter is replaced by another letter, number, or symbol

**symbol** something that stands for something else

**tachygraphy** another name for shorthand, a system for rapid writing that uses symbols or abbreviations for letters, words, or phrases. It is often used for taking down dictation.

**telegram** written form of a message sent by telegraph wires

**telegraph** machine used to send messages in code electronically over wires; the telegraph was widely used from the mid-1800s to the mid-1900s

**telegrapher** person who sends messages using a telegraph

**telescope** device used to see far away objects up close

**traitor** someone who betrays his or her country or the trust of another person

**translate** to change something from one language or code to another

**transmit** to send something from one place to another

**transpose** to change the positions of things, as in the order of letters in a word

**transposition cipher** cipher that first mixes up the letters in plaintext, then enciphers them

# More Books to Read

Bailly, Sharon. *Pass It On!* Brookfield, Conn.: Millbrook Press, 1995.

*Code Busters: Crack and Create Your Own Ciphers and Secret Codes.* Laguna Hills, Calif.: Walter Foster, 2002.

Fowler, Mark. *Codes & Ciphers.* Tulsa, Okla.: EDC Publications, 1995.

Miller, Marvin. *How to Write and Decode Secret Messages.* New York: Scholastic Paperbacks, 1998.

O'Brien, Eileen, with Dana Riddel. *Secret Codes.* Tulsa, Okla.: EDC Publishing, 1997.

Weller, Janet. *Messages in Code.* Danbury, Conn.: Franklin Watts, 1998.

## Answers to codes

page 32: CAN YOU READ THIS?, HIDE THE KEY
page 35: DID YOU PASS THE TEST?
page 39: DID YOU PASS THE TEST?

# Index